KU-316-634

The RAVENSWOOD Leisure, Recreation and Tourism Series

Case Studies in
FINANCIAL CONTROL and PERFORMANCE MEASUREMENT
in LEISURE and RECREATION MANAGEMENT

*with suggested answers*

D J Naylor and C Christian

RAVENSWOOD PUBLICATIONS LIMITED
35 Windsor Road, London N7 6JG

17 0158357 4

LEEDS METROPOLITAN
UNIVERSITY LIBRARY
1701583574
KLB
511614
790.069 NAY
28-1-97  £12.50

Published 1993

by

Ravenswood Publications Limited
35 Windsor Road
London   N7 6JG
England

ISBN 0 901812 73 0 soft cover

Cover design by G H Creative Group

A catalogue record for this book is available from the British
Library.

© Ravenswood Publications Limited 1992

All rights reserved

The right of Denise J Naylor and Clare Christian to be identified
as authors of this work has been asserted by them in accordance
with the Copyright Designs and Patents Act 1988.

No part of this publication may be reproduced or transmitted, in
any form or by any means, electronic, mechanical, photocopying,
recording or otherwise, without the written permission of the
publisher.

PREFACE

This is a companion volume to the case studies in financial
decision making published in 1992.

Once investment decisions have been taken, managers need to
evaluate the outcomes of their decisions.  The cases chosen are
representative of (mainly) outdoor leisure and recreation
activities available; as before we were spoilt for choice of
activities to cover.  As in the financial decision making case
studies, each solution is based on one set of numerical
assumptions.  The reader is invited to experiment with a range
of assumptions to see the effect upon results.  Budgeting and
performance measurement are arts which improve with practice.
Space has limited us to nine cases in which we show a range of
budgeting and performance measurement practices.

Denise Naylor BSc(Hons), FCA        Clare Christian BA, DipMS
March 1993


ACKNOWLEDGEMENTS

Thanks are due to Damon Guy and Steve Plumb for advice on
specific case studies.

CONTENTS

FINANCIAL CONTROL and PERFORMANCE MEASUREMENT
in LEISURE and RECREATION MANAGEMENT

## Kiddersdale Park

Following the process of Compulsory Competitive Tendering and tender evaluation the leisure company Country Pursuits Ltd has won the four year contract to run KIDDERSDALE PARK. The Park is a leisure and tourism park attracting both local residents and visitors from a wide catchment area. Country Pursuits Ltd submitted their bid for the management contract on the basis of a 32% recovery rate. Any income raised over and above the targets submitted will be split between the Contractor (80%) and Client (20%) so Country Pursuits has an incentive to increase the revenue raised.

The following are three proposals for the use of the Park but due to the insufficiency of funds for capital expenditure either by Country Pursuits Ltd or Kiddersdale District Council only one development can be embarked upon initially although outline planning permission has been given to all three proposals. All prices and costs are based on recent research.

### Proposal 1 - Crazy Golf

| | |
|---|---|
| Price (per round) | Adults - £1.50<br>Junior - £1.00 |
| Open | 6 months daily |
| Usage | 60 tickets/day<br>50% of users are adults |
| Repairs and maintenance | £115/week of opening |
| Ticket printing | 4.5 pence/100 |

One member of staff is required an average of 10 hours per day at £4 per hour to operate the course.

### Proposal 2 - Childrens Train

| | |
|---|---|
| Price/ride | 80 pence/child |
| Open | 26 weekends and Summer school holidays<br>(53 days) |
| Occupancy | Maximum = 15 children/trip<br>Average = 10 children/trip<br>Average 10 trips/day |
| Repairs and maintenance | £1.90/trip |
| Ticket printing | 4.5 pence/100 |

One member of staff is required six hours each day (£4 per hour).

# Kiddersdale Park

## Proposal 3 – All Terrain Vehicle Track

Price/30 minute session £5

Open 26 weekends and Summer school holidays (53 days)

Usage 12 ATV's available
Saturdays average 10 ATV's used/session average 5 sessions
Sundays average 10 ATV's used/session average 10 sessions
School hols average 5 ATV's used/session average 4 sessions/day

Repairs and maintenance (includes fuel) Average £1.80/ATV/session

Ticket printing – due to the rules and disclaimer being printed on them each ticket costs 8 pence.

Adequate supervision of the use of the vehicles and the track requires 3 staff members for 8 hours per day (£4 per hour) but also a mechanic has to spend one day (8 hours) per week of opening repairing the vehicles (£14/hour).

## REQUIRED

a) Which of the three proposed attractions is the best one to introduce into Kiddersdale Park?

Show annual operational budgets and recovery rates for each proposal.

   i) assuming that capital expenditure will be met from the Kiddersdale District Council Capital Budget (client side)

   ii) assuming that Country Pursuits Limited is responsible for funding all capital expenditure.

---

b) What other general management aspects should Country Pursuits consider before taking the final decision?

---

c) Country Pursuits Limited has been approached by Turinall Tracks Limited which is already managing ATV courses for other local authorities paying them either a lump sum annually or an agreed percentage of income.

In light of your advice in part (a), should Country Pursuits accept a lump sum of £1,000 or 5% of the income from the new ATV course?

Highlight the key points for consideration.

---

IGNORE TAXATION.

## Wigmarsh Waters

WIGMARSH WATERS is an urban based area of amenity land which attracts 300,000 visitors annually. Facilities include lakes offering various watersports which are complemented by cafes, a childrens play area, nature reserve and numerous picnic areas with fixed tables and benches.

Wigmarsh Waters is owned and subsidised by the Farleigh Metropolitan Borough Council and is run by the leisure DSO. As part of its preparation for CCT the management team have divided the operation into 4 cost centres:-

Water based Activity School

Rowing Lake

Grounds Maintenance and Horticulture

Premises and car parks

and apportioned the expenditure and revenue budgets accordingly.

In order to achieve the overall recovery rate of 55% stated in their successful bid the Manager, Judy Haslett, is devolving responsibility for the four cost centre budgets and their respective recovery rates.

### Expenditure · COST CENTRE ALLOCATIONS

| Total £ | | Activity School | Rowing Lake | Grounds | Premises |
|---|---|---|---|---|---|
| 72000 | Salaries | 35% | 10% | 35% | 20% |
| 76800 | Wages | 29% | 14% | 41% | 16% |
| 45600 | Maintenance | 18% | 3% | 65% | 14% |
| 14400 | Renewals | 72% | 28% | - | - |
| 31200 | Overheads | 6% | 4% | 5% | 85% |
| 240000 | | | | | |

### Income

| | | Activity School | Rowing Lake | Grounds | Premises |
|---|---|---|---|---|---|
| 31680 | Tuition | 100% | - | - | - |
| 72600 | Hiring of Equipment | 10% | 24% | 3% | 63% |
| 27720 | Lake/land use | 23% | - | 75% | 2% |
| 132000 | | | | | |

Rowing lake usage - annual

| Pedalos | 2700 hires |
|---|---|
| Boats | 3750 hires |

## Wigmarsh Waters

REQUIRED

a) Calculate the anticipated percentage recovery rate for each of the four cost centres in Wigmarsh Waters.

_____

b) How much (on average) would each visitor need to spend on each visit for Wigmarsh Waters to break even on an annual basis? Comment on your result.

_____

c) i) Judy Haslett believes that the Rowing lake could recover 90% of its expenditure. Using the information provided calculate what prices should be charged to achieve this target, assuming that rowing boat hire contributes 80% of the Rowing lake's income.

   ii) What other factors should Judy Haslett consider before implementing this pricing structure?

_____

## Patchett Wildlife Park

Christopher Boyd has recently inherited an area of land about 5 miles from a major motorway. He is intending to develop the land into a wildlife park which would primarily aim to be a family attraction with an educational basis. Mr Boyd has employed consultants to investigate the feasibility of the project and they have produced the following figures:-

Initial cost of the development including capital repayments and interest spread over 4 years = £640,000.

|  | Year 1 | Year 2 | Year 3 | Year 4 |
|---|---|---|---|---|
| Annual operating costs including depreciation | £400,000 | £525,000 | £575,000 | £630,000 |
| Annual visitor nos (000's) | | | | |
| Adult | 120 | 160 | 170 | 185 |
| Children | 80 | 90 | 120 | 140 |

## REQUIRED

a) What charges should be set for adults and children, if the child entry fee is 50% that of the adult entry fee, for the Wildlife Park to break even on an annual basis, covering all costs including costs relating to capital expenditure?

---

b) i) What would be the budgeted profit or loss if the charges were set at:

Adult £3.00
Child £2.50?

ii) What return on investment does this policy show?

---

c) Mr Boyd realises that there are other ways of raising revenue within the Wildlife Park and intends to introduce a merchandising outlet in year 2. The effect would be an overall increase in the operating costs of 8% annually. Items for sale would be priced at an average mark-up of 150% on cost price.

How much extra would each visitor have to spend to make this project worthwhile?

---

## Patchett Wildlife Park

d) Following the demise of various other wildlife parks and zoos Mr Boyd believes it may be necessary to introduce a series of educational and interpretive initiatives to encourage young visitors. The scheme includes a classroom, planting schemes, a monkey cage and guided trails and would cause an increase in operating costs of 15%. The initial cost will be spread over 4 years and amounts to £60,000 in total.

   i) How many visitors must the Patchett Wildlife Park attract in the first year to cover all costs including the proposed educational scheme? Assume the entry fees will be those suggested in (b) above.

   ii) Show the difference, if any, between this break-even target for number of visitors in the first year and the visitor numbers estimated by the consultant for the same period.

   What recommendations would you make to Mr Boyd on the basis of your appraisal of the educational scheme?

---

e) A second development possibility open to Mr Boyd is to introduce commercial attractions including "white knuckle" rides for an initial capital investment of £1 million and an estimated 40% increase in annual operating costs over the consultant's figures.

   Using the consultant's estimate of annual visitor numbers, calculate the revised charges needed to achieve the profit target shown in (b). For this proposal assume the child entry fee will be set at 50% of the adult entry fee.

---

## Vale Park Golf Driving Range

Broadvale Metropolitan Borough is planning to open to the public a newly built golf driving range with 20 driving bays on 1st April next. Land adjacent to VALE PARK, already owned and managed by the council, is offered for sale at £55,000 and the Borough Surveyor advises that access and other necessary estate works will cost a further £40,000. Both of these sums have been earmarked in this year's Capital Budget and this expenditure has been authorised by the Finance Committee for spending before 31st March next.

The Finance Committee, at the same meeting, approved a Revenue Budget for next financial year for the golf driving range containing the following details:

1.  A local supplier has quoted £110 per bay for netting; payable in advance of the opening.

2.  The purchasing department estimates that golf clubs for hire can be obtained for a total of £3,000 provided payment is made before 31st March next.

3.  Advance publicity and marketing costs of £500 will be paid in March, immediately prior to the opening.

4.  Maintenance of grounds and nets will be provided by existing staff at an extra cost of £60 per week.

5.  On-going advertising and marketing costs are estimated at £1,500 a year.

6.  Qualified coaching staff will be employed to supervise the driving range and to hold coaching sessions. This will add a total of £20,000 a year to staff costs. The £20,000 includes NI and employers pension contributions.

7.  Revenue is estimated:

| | £ per week |
|---|---|
| Jan, Feb, Nov, Dec | 450 |
| Mar, Apl, May, Oct | 800 |
| Jun, Jul, Aug, Sep | 1,100 |

    The driving range will close only for Christmas Week.

8.  Vale Park golf driving range is planned with a working life of ten years before complete re-laying will be required.

## REQUIRED

a)  Calculate the Payback Period for the Driving Range (in months).

---

## Vale Park Golf Driving Range

b) Calculate the net present value (NPV) of the Driving Range using a discount rate (cost of capital) of 8%.

---

c) Show the effect on the NPV of the Driving Range if the cost of capital rises to 10%.

What does this tell you about the project?

---

d) Prepare a cash budget (cash flow forecast) covering the next financial year's Revenue Estimates on a monthly basis.

NOTE: Spread costs and revenues evenly unless given other timings of cash flows.

---

e) The Broadvale Metropolitan Borough Finance Committee has set a target of 100% annual recovery rate on Revenue Estimates for the Vale Park Driving Range. Calculate an estimated annual recovery rate(s) for the project, based on the figures given.

---

f) Identify key points for financial control arising from your results.

---

g) Highlight the differences in approach to the feasibility of the Driving Range between a local authority manager and a manager of a contractor organisation bidding to operate the project within the current legal framework. What matters will be of similar importance to both managers?

---

IGNORE INFLATION

ASSUME THAT ALL CASH FLOWS ARISE AT THE END OF THE YEAR TO WHICH THEY RELATE.

---

The present value of £1, discounted at 8%, received at the end of Year 1 is £0.926; Year 2 is £0.857; Year 3 is £0.794; Year 4 is £0.735; Year 5 is £0.681; Year 6 is £0.630; Year 7 is £0.583; Year 8 is £0.540; Year 9 is £0.500; Year 10 is £0.463.

The present value of £1, discounted at 10%, received at the end of Year 1 is £0.909; Year 2 is £0.826; Year 3 is £0.751; Year 4 is £0.683; Year 5 is £0.621; Year 6 is £0.564; Year 7 is £0.513; Year 8 is £0.467; Year 9 is £0.424; Year 10 is £0.386.

**Salhaven Watersports Centre**

SALHAVEN WATERSPORTS CENTRE opened in 1977 and was refurbished by its owners Salhaven District Council in 1990. The management contract has been won by the Salhaven Direct Services Organisation (DSO) for a four-year period.

The Centre offers a wide range of outdoor watersport activities and is very popular within the community. Usage of the Centre is very high and in the summer months the Centre is almost always operating at full capacity. The Centre is open every day of the year, except Christmas Day.

The Centre manager is currently working on the Budgets for the next financial year and the following information is available from the first year of the contract.

1. **Salhaven Watersports Centre: expected outturn for latest financial year**

   | Revenue from activities | £ per week |
   |---|---|
   | Jan, Feb, Nov, Dec | 800 |
   | Mar, Apl, May, Oct | 3,100 |
   | Jun, Jul, Aug, Sep | 1,200 |

   Of this revenue, a total of £25,000 was invoiced to schools for their pupils' use and £3,600 was received from clubs for their members' use of facilities.

   Revenue from catering facilities is expected to total £14,000 for the full year.

2. **Salhaven Watersports Centre: draft expenditure account for latest financial year 1st April (previous) to 31st March (latest)**

   | Staff Costs | £ |
   |---|---|
   | Salaries, wages, NI | 100,000 |
   | Uniforms, wet suits etc | 1,000 |
   | Training | 2,000 |
   | | 103,000 |

   | Centre Operating Costs | |
   |---|---|
   | Energy costs | 30,000 |
   | Equipment new and replacement | 35,000 |
   | Insurances | 10,000 |
   | Office costs (post, telephone, printing, stationery etc) | 6,000 |
   | Provisions for bar and catering | 12,000 |
   | Repairs and maintenance | 8,000 |
   | | 101,000 |

   | Central Services Costs | |
   |---|---|
   | Finance | 3,000 |
   | Legal | 500 |
   | Management and administration | 9,000 |
   | Marketing | 7,500 |
   | | 20,000 |
   | TOTAL GROSS EXPENDITURE | 224,000 |

## Salhaven Watersports Centre

At the present time the Centre manager has information that salaries and wages will rise by 2%; energy costs will rise by 5% and insurance costs will rise by 10% in the next financial year.

Service Level Agreements include clauses that fix the annual costs for the duration of the contract.

3.    **The Management Contract**

Salhaven District Council retains the right to set the pricing policy of the Watersports Centre; they specify that price rises each year must be limited to a 3% increase on the preceding year.

The DSO has an annual gross expenditure target of £250,000 which must not be exceeded.    Central Services costs are subject to separately negotiated Service Level Agreements. Salhaven Council has set a target recovery rate on Revenue Account of 50% to be achieved by the end of the contract.

4.    **New Activities**

The Centre manager would like to see new activities introduced, but because of the financial targets set, any new activity must be capable of reaching break-even within the first two years of its introduction.

One new activity under consideration is the introduction of windsurfing for two sessions per week (a session lasts for 3 hours).    A supplier has quoted an inclusive cost of £3,000 for equipment expected to have a five-year life before being scrapped. Additional staff would be needed at a gross cost of £8 per hour and the anticipated average revenue from a session is £40.

## REQUIRED

a)    Prepare suitable performance measures for the Centre for each year of the DSO contract, to set the framework for the Operating Budgets.

---

b)    Prepare an Operating Budget (Revenue and Expenditure) for the next financial year.

Discuss how the Centre might achieve its target recovery rate.

---

c)    Evaluate the proposal to introduce windsurfing.

---

## Oxley Sports and Social Club

OXLEY SPORTS AND SOCIAL CLUB was set up as a charitable trust 25 years ago. The trust was bequeathed a large property and surrounding grounds by a local dignitary and with the aid of Council grants, and an appeal for funds the trustees were able to provide a competitive range of indoor and outdoor facilities. Membership is necessary to use the facilities and the Club was very popular in its early years. During the 1980s however, the perception of users changed and the Club became seen as out-of-date and with little scope for social functions apart from the annual dinner and dance.

In 1989, the trustees commenced a major refurbishment of the premises with the aim of upgrading most of the facilities and a full-time Secretary was recruited to take responsibility for operations and report direct to the committee of management. The trust was able to raise a loan of £750,000 on preferential terms. During the following two years, the Club struggled to meet the interest payments on the loan in the face of falling membership, but recently the Club is gaining in popularity with both membership and use of the facilities increasing year by year.

Summarised financial accounts of Oxley Sports and Social Club are shown below:

### Summarised Balance Sheet

|  | Latest Year £000 | Previous Year £000 |
|---|---|---|
| **Fixed Assets** | | |
| Land and buildings (at cost) | 1,093 | 1,093 |
| Equipment & Fixtures (net) | 556 | 687 |
|  | 1,649 | 1,780 |
| **Current Assets** | | |
| Stock | 30 | 32 |
| Debtors | 55 | 50 |
| Cash | 44 | 4 |
|  | 129 | 86 |
| Creditors: amounts falling due within one year (1) | 372 | 490 |
| Net Current Assets/(Liabilities) | (243) | (404) |
| Total assets less current liabilities | 1,406 | 1,376 |
| Creditors: amounts falling due after more than one year (2) | 950 | 1,000 |
|  | 456 | 376 |

## Oxley Sports and Social Club

|  | £000 | £000 |
|---|---:|---:|
| Capital and reserves | | |
| Capital fund: | | |
| Balance at 1st April previous | 586 | 586 |
| Profit and loss account | (150) | (230) |
| | 436 | 356 |
| Repairs and renewals fund | 20 | 20 |
| | 456 | 376 |

| (1) Creditors | Latest Year £000 | Previous Year £000 |
|---|---:|---:|
| Overdraft (unsecured) | 171 | 240 |
| Trade creditors | 78 | 90 |
| Social security and other taxes | 40 | 45 |
| Other creditors | 83 | 115 |
| | 372 | 490 |

| (2) Creditors | | |
|---|---:|---:|
| Bank Loan | 712 | 750 |
| Loan from Oxley Council | 238 | 250 |
| | 950 | 1,000 |

### Summarised profit and loss account

| | | Latest Year £000 | | Previous Year £000 |
|---|---:|---:|---:|---:|
| Turnover | | 1,564 | | 1,432 |
| Other operating income | | 250 | | 210 |
| | | 1,814 | | 1,642 |
| Staff costs | 912 | | 894 | |
| Depreciation | 131 | | 127 | |
| Other operating costs | 606 | | 609 | |
| | | 1,649 | | 1,630 |
| Operating profit | | 165 | | 12 |
| Interest payable | | 85 | | 90 |
| Profit/(loss) for the financial year | | 80 | | (78) |
| Balance at 1st April previous | | (230) | | (152) |
| Balance at 31st March latest | | (150) | | (230) |

## Oxley Sports and Social Club

Budgets for the next year are being prepared and the Secretary has been asked by the trustees at the latest committee of management to aim to turn the existing accumulated deficit into a surplus (profit) and to repay the overdraft in its entirety.

At the present time the Secretary has information that staff costs will rise by 3% and the interest payable will be reduced by 10%. The Secretary's plan is to increase turnover by 10% both by increasing charges for facilities at the Club and by increasing the number of users. In order to achieve this plan, a significant marketing budget will be provided for the first time in the history of the Club and this will have the effect of increasing the budget for other operating costs by 8% in the next year. All other items in the profit and loss account will be budgeted for next year at latest year amounts.

Apart from the committee's target of reducing the overdraft, all other items of working capital are to be budgeted to stay in the same ratio to turnover as shown in the latest accounts. The bank loan is to be reduced to £680,000 and the loan from Oxley Council is to be reduced to £222,000 by next balance sheet date. The Secretary is budgeting for no change in the balances on capital fund and repairs and renewals fund.

### REQUIRED

a) Prepare a budgeted profit and loss account for next year and a budgeted balance sheet as at the end of next year.

---

b) Outline key points for financial control at the Club which will help the Secretary to achieve the budget prepared.

---

## Bogood Breweries

The directors of BOGOOD BREWERIES plc, a company which specialises in the brewing and marketing of beer in the UK and Europe, are seeking to upgrade production facilities and introduce new brands. They are considering making a capital investment of £500,000 in fixed assets, financed by an addition to their existing bank loan secured on the new assets at an initial rate (variable) of 12.5% per annum.

Summarised financial accounts of Bogood Breweries plc are shown below:

### Summarised Balance Sheet

|  | Latest Year £000 | Previous Year £000 |
|---|---|---|
| **Fixed Assets** | | |
| Land and buildings (at revaluation) | 2,774 | 2,357 |
| Equipment & Fixtures (net) | 432 | 395 |
| | 3,206 | 2,752 |
| **Current Assets** | | |
| Stock | 155 | 206 |
| Debtors | 276 | 251 |
| Investments (at cost) (1) | 352 | 448 |
| Cash | 80 | 69 |
| | 863 | 974 |
| Creditors: amounts falling due within one year (2) | 954 | 897 |
| Net Current Assets/(Liabilities) | (91) | 77 |
| Total assets less current liabilities | 3,115 | 2,829 |
| Creditors: amounts falling due after more than one year (3) | 1,150 | 1,000 |
| | 1,965 | 1,829 |
| **Capital and reserves** | | |
| Called up share capital (£1 shares) | 600 | 600 |
| Revaluation reserve | 580 | 580 |
| Profit and loss account | 785 | 649 |
| | 1,965 | 1,829 |

### NOTES

(1) Investments
   Latest year: short term deposits £150,000 and listed investments at market value £242,000.
   Previous year: short term deposits £195,000 and listed investments at market value £270,000.

- 14 -

## Bogood Breweries

| (2) | Creditors | Latest Year £000 | Previous Year £000 |
|---|---|---|---|
| | Trade creditors | 330 | 316 |
| | Corporation tax | 90 | 110 |
| | Proposed dividend | 25 | 25 |
| | Bank overdraft (unsecured) | 509 | 446 |
| | | 954 | 897 |

| (3) | Creditors | | |
|---|---|---|---|
| | 13% Debenture 2005 | 1,000 | 1,000 |
| | Bank Loan (secured) | 150 | - |
| | | 1,150 | 1,000 |

### Summarised profit and loss account

| | Latest Year £000 | Previous Year £000 |
|---|---|---|
| Turnover | 2,842 | 2,305 |
| Trading profit | 341 | 270 |
| Interest (net) | 76 | 49 |
| Profit before taxation | 265 | 221 |
| Taxation | 90 | 72 |
| Profit after taxation | 175 | 149 |
| Dividend | 39 | 36 |
| Retained profit | 136 | 113 |

The company's debentures are currently trading at £98.50 and the ordinary share price is 182p.

Dividends are expected to grow at an annual rate of 6%. Bogood Breweries plc is subject to an effective corporate tax rate of 30%.

### Comparative data for Bogood Breweries industry (averages)

| | |
|---|---|
| Share price | 220 pence |
| Dividend yield | 6% |
| Net asset turnover | 0.75 times |
| Earnings per share | 35 pence |
| Gearing (total loans/shareholder's funds) | 75% |
| Acid test | 0.9:1 |
| Interest cover | 7 times |
| Dividend cover | 50% |
| Return on sales (profit before tax and interest/sales) | 10% |

## Bogood Breweries

REQUIRED

a)   Using the summarised accounts of Bogood Breweries plc and the comparative industry ratios; calculate for the latest year and for the previous year and compare with industry averages:-

   i)   four commonly-used measures of liquidity (or solvency): at least one short-term and at least one longer-term

   ii)  two commonly-used measures of profitability and

   iii) three commonly-used measures of performance for Bogood Breweries as a public limited company.

---

b)   Write a brief report to the management of Bogood Breweries plc highlighting trends in the company's performance.

---

c)   The directors expect the new investment of £500,000 to generate cash flows of £150,000 a year each year for five years. At the end of the five years the project will have no value.

   i)   Calculate the net present value (NPV) of the investment using a discount rate of 12%, based on the after-tax cash flows.

   ii)  The interest payable on the bank loan is variable. On the assumption that interest rates may rise within the period of this loan, should the directors undertake this investment? Why or why not?

---

d)   Write a brief report on the company from the point of view of the manager of the bank which has provided the finance for Bogood's loans and overdraft.

---

IGNORE INFLATION

ASSUME THAT ALL CASH FLOWS ARISE AT THE END OF THE YEAR TO WHICH THEY RELATE.

---

The present value of £1, discounted at 12%, received at the end of Year 1 is £0.893; Year 2 is £0.797; Year 3 is £0.712; Year 4 is £0.636; Year 5 is £0.567; Year 6 is £0.507.

**Abbey Farm Forest**

Ann and Graham Wright own Abbey Farm.  Their next door landowner died last year and, in order to settle his tax bill, his heirs have offered for sale the area of woodland and scrubland known locally as "ABBEY FARM FOREST" which is situated alongside the Wrights' farmland.

The Wrights are finding farming to be less and less profitable than in the past and are looking to diversify their business.  They propose to manage the woodland commercially and sell rights of access for recreation and sport.

Their preliminary investigations reveal:

1.   The land "Abbey Farm Forest" would cost £70,000, new fencing costing £15,000 and new signposting £2,000.  The Wrights would also take the opportunity to upgrade one of the farm vehicles to a newer model suitable for woodland management at a net cost (less trade-in value of old vehicle) of £20,000.  The investment will be financed from their savings.

2.   Additional maintenance and staffing costs of taking on Abbey Farm Forest will be £100 a week.

3.   The proposed programme for recreation and sport is:

| User | Access | Number of Weekends | Number of Days Mon-Fri |
|------|--------|--------------------|------------------------|
| Motor Cycle Rally Clubs | First & Third Weekends | 20 Open use 4 Events | |
| Horse Riding Clubs | Second & Fourth Weekends | 24 | |
| No access permitted | Varies | 4 | |
| Shooting Clubs | Varies | | 60 |
| Corporate hospitality days | Varies | | 60 |

4.   Proposed charges are:

**Motor Cycle Rally Clubs**

Club membership £25 per family.
Members pay £5 per day per motorcyclist for use.
Special Event £200 per weekend + £2 per rider.

**Horse Riding Clubs**

Annual licence fee of £100 payable in advance for access as permitted.

**Shooting Clubs**

Club membership £50 per person annually.

**Abbey Farm Forest**

**Corporate hospitality days**

Per capita charge of £20.

All charges for the recreation and sport programme will be payable direct to the Wrights who, together with their staff, will manage the programme.

The Wrights propose to sub-contract the management of corporate hospitality days to a specialist agent who will receive 75% of revenues and meet all costs of these activities.

5.  The following estimates of utilisation are based on the experience of other similar activities held in nearby counties and on the Wrights' own local knowledge.

**Motorcycle Rally Clubs**

Target club membership:     80 families
Members' open use weekends:  estimates are of between 30 and 50 riders each weekend

Members' special event weekends:

| Number of riders expected | Probability |
|---|---|
| 350 | 0.05 |
| 300 | 0.25 |
| 250 | 0.35 |
| 200 | 0.30 |
| 150 | 0.05 |

**Horse Riding Clubs**

There are 20 Clubs in the locality and the Wrights expect them all to apply for licences because most landowners in the district do not permit horse riding on their land and bridle paths are not numerous either.

**Shooting Clubs**

Target club membership: 100 members

**Corporate Hospitality**

Participants limited to a maximum of 60 on any one day.

| Number of players expected | Probability |
|---|---|
| 60 | 0.05 |
| 55 | 0.10 |
| 50 | 0.20 |
| 45 | 0.30 |
| 40 | 0.20 |
| 35 | 0.10 |
| 30 | 0.05 |

**Abbey Farm Forest**

6.    The annual costs of insurance, maintenance and timber
      management in Abbey Farm Forest will be covered by income
      from sales of timber products and development grants
      available to the Wrights under government policies for the
      countryside.  The only "profit" available to them will be
      from the recreation and sport programme.  They have set
      themselves a target annual profit of £12,000 which they
      would draw as salaries for managing the Forest Recreation
      and Sport Programme.

      The Wrights propose to run the recreation and sport
      programme for five years and then to re-consider the
      situation.

REQUIRED

a)    Prepare a budget for the first year of operation of the
      recreation and sport programme.

      Are Ann and Graham Wright likely to achieve their profit
      target?

      How vulnerable is their achievement to changes in expected
      results?

_____

b)    Prepare suitable ratios and performance measures for the
      recreation and sport programme.

_____

c)    Identify key points for financial control.

_____

## Topflight

The manager of the Leisure Division of Glenhall Limited, a successful tour operator, is planning the launch of TOPFLIGHT a 90-minute trip in an airship with champagne and refreshments included. The tour would be marketed to the corporate hospitality sector, with some trips on sale to the general public through advertising in the local press and on local radio. The proposal is to buy one airship with a viewing area to accommodate a maximum of twenty passengers served by three crew members. The external surfaces of the airship will be sold for advertising campaigns.

Negotiations with the local airport authority have resulted in outline permission for the airship to make one circuit a day. The number of flights required must be booked before the beginning of each flying season.

1.  Estimated costs of the project are as follows:

    |                                                                        | £         |                    |
    | ---------------------------------------------------------------------- | --------- | ------------------ |
    | Capital cost of the airship                                            | 1,200,000 | payable on delivery |
    | Cost of servicing, maintenance mooring rights and marketing costs      | 45,000    | per year           |
    | Cost of airship crew, ground staff and service facilities              | 90,000    | per year           |
    | Variable costs of food and beverages, airship fuel and oil             | 25        | per passenger      |

    The airship will have a working life of five years only. At the end of five years the airship is expected to have no scrap value.

2.  Estimated income from the project:

    a)  <u>From advertising</u>

        Advertising revenue is budgeted at £25,000 a year.

    b)  <u>From passengers taking the tour</u>

        The market research department has recommended advertising the tour at a price of £120 per passenger per flight. At that price they forecast customer demand of 4,500 passengers a year. They advise that every increase or decrease in the price by £20 will result in a corresponding decrease or increase respectively in demand of 500 passengers a year. At a price of £300 demand will be zero.

## Topflight

Market research has supplied the following estimates of capacity utilisation in the viewing area (eg a capacity of 90% means 18 passengers):

| Average capacity utilisation | Probability |
|---|---|
| 100% | 0.05 |
| 95% | 0.05 |
| 90% | 0.10 |
| 85% | 0.10 |
| 80% | 0.20 |
| 75% | 0.15 |
| 65% | 0.15 |
| 55% | 0.10 |
| 50% | 0.10 |

3. The latest published accounts of Glenhall Limited show an annual turnover (sales) of £30 million; profit before taxation of £7.5 million and net assets of £50 million.

Glenhall Limited uses the straight line method of providing for depreciation on its fixed assets. Assets are shown in the accounts at mid-year book values under the historical cost convention.

## REQUIRED

a) Using the market research information provided

   i) show the total cost function and the total revenue function for the project TOPFLIGHT;

   ii) calculate the price to be charged per passenger and the annual passenger demand which will produce maximum profits for Glenhall from TOPFLIGHT; and

   iii) show by means of flexible budgets that profits will be maximised at this price and annual number of passengers.

---

b) Using the estimated price and estimated annual passenger demand information from (a), how many flights should Glenhall book in advance for its first flying season?

---

## Topflight

c)   The primary objective of the directors is to maximise the
     profitability of the company.  Every divisional manager has
     been set a target of increasing the return on investment
     (ROI) reported by their division year on year and
     participation in a bonus scheme is dependant upon results.

     The manager of Glenhall's Leisure Division who will operate
     the tour TOPFLIGHT, if it goes ahead, currently reports a
     ROI of 17%.

     i)    Calculate an annual ROI for TOPFLIGHT for each year of
           its life and overall.  Use the accounting methods
           employed in the company.

     ii)   Calculate the net present value of the project from
           the point of view of the company as a whole.

     iii)  Calculate the net present value of the project from
           the point of view of Leisure Division.

     What decisions do you think will be reached?

     Discuss their effects on the returns to the shareholders of
     Glenhall Limited.

---

IGNORE INFLATION

ASSUME THAT ALL CASH FLOWS ARISE AT THE END OF THE YEAR TO WHICH
THEY RELATE.

---

The present value of £1, discounted at 15%, received at the end
of Year 1 is £0.870; Year 2 is £0.756; Year 3 is £0.658; Year 4
is £0.572; Year 5 is £0.497.

The present value of £1, discounted at 17%, received at the end
of Year 1 is £0.855; Year 2 is £0.730; Year 3 is £0.624; Year 4
is £0.534; Year 5 is £0.456.

**Kiddersdale Park**

a)   Proposal 1 – Crazy Golf

Income

| | | | |
|---|---|---|---|
| 50% adult | 5475 x £1.50 | = | £ 8212.50 |
| 50% junior | 5475 x £1.00 | = | £ 5475.00 |
| 26 weeks x 60 tickets/day | 10950 | | £13687.50 |

Expenditure

| | | | |
|---|---|---|---|
| Repairs & maintenance | 26 weeks x £115 per week | = | £ 2990.00 |
| Tickets | 10950 entrances x 4.5p/100 | = | £    4.93 |
| Staffing | 10 hours per day x £4 per hour x 365/2 | = | £ 7300.00 |
| | | | £10294.93 |

Profit          =     £3392.57

Recovery Rate   =     133%

Proposal 2 – Childrens Train

Income

105 days (52 weekend days + 53 hols days)   x   10 trips   x   10 children   x   80 pence   =   £8400

Expenditure

| | | | |
|---|---|---|---|
| Repairs & maintenance | 105 days x 10 trips/day x £1.90 | = | £1995.00 |
| Tickets | 105 days x 10 trips x 10 children x 4.5p/100 | = | £   4.73 |
| Staffing | 6 hours per day x 105 days x £4 per hour | = | £2520.00 |
| | | | £4519.73 |

Profit          =     £3880.27

Recovery Rate   =     186%

# Kiddersdale Park

## Proposal 3 - ATV Track

### Income

| | | | | | | | | |
|---|---|---|---|---|---|---|---|---|
| Saturdays | 5 sessions | x | 10 ATV's | x | 26 | = | 1300 sessions | |
| Sundays | 10 sessions | x | 10 ATV's | x | 26 | = | 2600 sessions | |
| School hols | 4 sessions | x | 5 ATV's | x | 53 | = | 1060 sessions | |
| | | | | | | | 4960 sessions | |
| | | | | | | x | £5 | |
| | | | | | | = | £24800 | |

### Expenditure

| | | | | | | |
|---|---|---|---|---|---|---|
| Repairs & maintenance | £1.80 | x | 4960 sessions | | = | £ 8928.00 |
| Tickets | 8 pence | x | 4960 sessions | | = | £  396.80 |
| Staff - operational: | 8 hours per day x 3 staff x 105 days x £4 per hour | | | | = | £10080.00 |
| mechanic | 8 hours per day x 26 weeks x £14 per hour | | | | = | £ 2912.00 |
| | | | | | | £12992.00 |
| | | | | Total expenditure | = | £22316.80 |

**Profit** = £2483.20

**Recovery rate** = £111%

Childrens train is therefore the most profitable and has highest recovery rate.

## Kiddersdale Park

b)   The management team might consider the three proposals in terms of:

-   weather dependency affecting the number of days on which opening is feasible
-   effect on usage of other facilities within the Park
-   effect on image of Park
-   the potential market for each proposal
-   possible impact on the environment including noise, litter, visual impact
-   life expectancy of the investment.

They should also look at the possibility of a franchisee taking the risk in return for an income share or lump sum.

c)   5% of ATV tracks expected income is £1240 which is not dramatically higher than £1000 lump sum so Country Pursuits Ltd should look carefully at:

-   reliability of expected income figures
-   poor weather or other uncontrollable factors affecting usage
-   timing of payments and Turinall Tracks reputation.

# Wigmarsh Waters

a)

| | Activity School £ | Rowing Lake £ | Grounds £ | Premises £ |
|---|---|---|---|---|
| **Expenditure** | | | | |
| Salaries | 25200 | 7200 | 25200 | 14400 |
| Wages | 22272 | 10752 | 31488 | 12288 |
| Maintenance | 8208 | 1368 | 29640 | 6384 |
| Renewals | 10368 | 4032 | – | – |
| Overheads | 1872 | 1248 | 1560 | 26520 |
| **Income** | | | | |
| Tuition | 31680 | – | – | – |
| Hiring of equipment | 7260 | 17424 | 2178 | 45738 |
| Lake/land use | 6375.60 | – | 20790 | 554.40 |
| Total expenditure | 67920 | 24600 | 87888 | 59592 |
| Total income | 45315.60 | 17424 | 22968 | 46292.40 |
| **Recovery rate** | **67%** | **71%** | **26%** | **78%** |

b)

$$\frac{\text{Total expenditure}}{\text{Annual visitor nos}} = \frac{£240000}{300000} = \textbf{80 pence per visitor}$$

This figure is comparatively very low for a day attraction but WIGMARSH WATERS does not at present charge any entry fee so the figure cannot be judged in direct comparison with attractions which do so.

## Wigmarsh Waters

c)  i)

| | |
|---|---|
| Total expenditure | £24600 |
| Income to recover 90% | £22140 |
| Rowing boat income | £17712 |
| Pedalos income | £ 4428 |

Therefore prices need to be:

Rowing boats  $\dfrac{£17712}{3750}$  =  £4.72  **(say £4.75)**

Pedalos  $\dfrac{£4428}{2700}$  =  £1.64  **(say £1.70)**

ii)  – Economic climate and current pricing.
   – Effect of pricing on usage – optimal pricing.
   – Competitors pricing and that of other facilities within Wigmarsh Waters.
   – Differential pricing (eg peak and off peak or adults and children and group rates)
   – Weather dependency and climatic changes.

## Patchett Wildlife Park

### a)

|                                            | Year 1 £000s | Year 2 £000s | Year 3 £000s | Year 4 £000s |
|--------------------------------------------|-------------|-------------|-------------|-------------|
| Capital Expenditure                        | 160         | 160         | 160         | 160         |
| Operating costs                            | 400         | 525         | 575         | 630         |
| Gross expenditure                          | 560         | 685         | 735         | 790         |
|                                            | ÷           | ÷           | ÷           | ÷           |
| Weighted average expected visitor numbers (000s) (1) | 320 | 410 | 460 | 510 |
| Break-even entry fee:                      |             |             |             |             |
| **Adult**                                  | £3.50       | £3.34       | £3.20       | £3.10       |
| **Child**                                  | £1.75       | £1.67       | £1.60       | £1.55       |

(1) With a child entry fee set at 50% of the adult entry fee a weighted average of visitor numbers is calculated:

eg   Year 1 [120,000 Adult x 2] + [80,000 Child x 1] gives 320,000 weighted average visitor numbers.

Check: 120,000 Adult @ £3.50 = £420,000
       80,000 Child @ £1.75 = £140,000
       Projected income        £560,000  which covers Gross Expenditure

### b) i)

|                              | Year 1 £000s | Year 2 £000s | Year 3 £000s | Year 4 £000s |
|------------------------------|-------------|-------------|-------------|-------------|
| Projected Income (2)         | 560         | 705         | 810         | 905         |
| Projected Expenditure (as in (a)) | 560    | 685         | 735         | 790         |
| Profit                       | NIL         | 20          | 75          | 115         |

(2) eg Year 1  120,000 Adult @ £3.00 = £360,000
                80,000 Child @ £2.50 = £200,000
                Projected Income        £560,000

Total profit earned during the first four years (assuming no dividend payouts and all profit re-invested in the Park) is £210,000.

# Patchett Wildlife Park

**b)** **ii)** The average return on investment during this period is

$$= \frac{\text{Average profit} \times 100\%}{\text{Average Investment}} = \frac{£210,000 \div 4 \text{ years}}{£640,000 \div 2 \text{ years}} = \frac{£52,500 \text{ average annual profit}}{£320,000 \text{ average investment value}} = 16.4\%$$

This assumes that the investment cost of £640,000 is fully written-off over the four years.

**c)**

|  | Year 2 £000s | Year 3 £000s | Year 4 £000s |
|---|---|---|---|
| Original Estimated Operating Cost (as in (a)) | 525 | 575 | 630 |
| Revised Estimate | 567 | 621 | 680 |
| Additional Cost | 42 | 46 | 50 |
|  | ÷ | ÷ | ÷ |
| Expected visitor numbers (000s) (3) | 250 | 290 | 325 |
| Additional Cost per visitor | 17 pence | 16 pence | 15 pence |
| At a mark-up of 150% on cost this implies sales per visitor of | 28 pence | 27 pence | 25 pence |

$\frac{108}{100}$

Check: 250,000 visitors spending 28p    £70,000

Less: cost price of goods sold $\frac{100}{250}$    £28,000

Profit    £42,000

## Patchett Wildlife Park

**d) i) Educational Scheme Proposal**

| | Year 1 £000s | Year 2 £000s | Year 3 £000s | Year 4 £000s |
|---|---|---|---|---|
| Gross expenditure from original estimates (see (a)) | 560 | 685 | 735 | 790 |
| Additional initial investment £60,000 ÷ 4 years | 15 | 15 | 15 | 15 |
| Additional operating cost £400,000 x 15% | 60 | £525,000 x 15% 78.75 | £575,000 x 15% 86.25 | £630,000 x 15% 94.5 |
| Revised gross expenditure | 635 | 778.75 | 836.25 | 899.5 |

| | Adult | Child |
|---|---|---|
| Proposed entry fee (see (b)) | £3.00 x 60% | £2.50 x 40% |

Weighted average entry fee = £1.80 + £1.00 = £2.80

Break-even = £Total fixed cost ÷ £Average entry fee
= £635,000 ÷ £2.80
= 226,786 visitors in total

| In estimated proportions | Adult | Child |
|---|---|---|
| | 226,786 x 60% | 226,786 x 40% |
| | **136,072** | **90,714** |

Check: 136,072 Adult entries @ £3.00 = £408,216
90,714 Child entries @ £2.50 = £226,785
£635,001

# Patchett Wildlife Park

## d) ii) Visitors Year 1

| | Consultant's Estimate | Break-Even Target | Difference |
|---|---|---|---|
| Adult | 120,000 | 136,072 | 16,072 |
| Child | 80,000 | 90,714 | 10,714 |
| | 200,000 | 226,786 | 26,786 SHORTFALL |

The options available to the Park include raising entry fees, attracting larger numbers of visitors or a larger proportion of adult visitors, or any combination of these actions. There may be an increase in operating costs if Mr Boyd decides to increase marketing to attract more visitors. One or more of these options will have to be implemented if the educational scheme is to be included in the Park.

## e) Commercial attractions proposal

| | Year 1 £000s | Year 2 £000s | Year 3 £000s | Year 4 £000s |
|---|---|---|---|---|
| Gross expenditure from original estimates (see (a)) | 560 | 685 | 735 | 790 |
| Additional initial investment £1m ÷ 4 | 250 | 250 | 250 | 250 |
| Additional operating cost | | | | |
| £400,000 x 40% ÷ 4 | 160 | | | |
| £525,000 x 40% | | 210 | | |
| £575,000 x 40% | | | 230 | |
| £630,000 x 40% | | | | 252 |
| Average profit target £210,000 ÷ 4 | 52.5 | 52.5 | 52.5 | 52.5 |
| Revised gross expenditure | 1,022.5 | 1,197.5 | 1,267.5 | 1,344.5 |
| | ÷ | ÷ | ÷ | ÷ |
| Weighted average expected visitor numbers (000s) (1) | 320 | 410 | 460 | 510 |
| **Required entry fee:** | | | | |
| Adult | £6.40 | £5.84 | £5.52 | £5.27 |
| Child | £3.20 | £2.92 | £2.76 | £2.64 |

(1) With a child entry fee set at 50% of the adult entry fee a weighted average of visitor numbers is calculated:

eg Year 1 [120,000 Adult x 2] + [80,000 Child x 1] gives 320,000 weighted average visitor numbers.

Check:  120,000 Adult @ £6.40 = £ 768,000
        80,000 Child @ £3.20 = £ 256,000
        Projected Income    £1,024,000  (differences due to rounding of entry fee charges)

# Vale Park Golf Driving Range

a) Payback Period (in months)

| | £ | |
|---|---|---|
| Items in Capital Budget only | 95,000 | |
| Set-up costs in Revenue Budget | 5,700 | |
| TOTAL CASH OUTLAY | 100,700 | |

Annual Cash INFLOWS (net)    15,680    see working

PAYBACK    $\dfrac{£100,700}{£15,680}$    =    6.422 years

=    **77 months**    (6 yrs 5 months)

Working:

| Annual Revenue Estimates | | £ |
|---|---|---|
| (see cash flow qu. 6) | | |
| 16 weeks @ £ 450 p.w. | = | 7,200 |
| 18 weeks @ £ 800 p.w. | = | 14,400 |
| 17 weeks @ £1,100 p.w. | = | 18,700 |
| 51 | | 40,300 |

| Annual Expenditure Estimates | £ |
|---|---|
| Maintenance 52 weeks* @ £60 | 3,120 |
| Advertising | 1,500 |
| Staff | 20,000 |
| | 24,620 |

Annual Estimated Surplus £15,680

\* assume that maintenance continues during closure week

b&c) NPVs

| Year | Cash Flows £ | PV @ 8% | PV £ | PV @ 10% | PV £ |
|---|---|---|---|---|---|
| 0 | - 100,700 | 1.000 | -100,700 | 1.000 | -100,700 |
| 1 | + 15,680 | 0.926 | + 14,520 | 0.909 | + 14,253 |
| 2 | + 15,680 | 0.857 | + 13,438 | 0.826 | + 12,952 |
| 3 | + 15,680 | 0.794 | + 12,450 | 0.751 | + 11,776 |
| 4 | + 15,680 | 0.735 | + 11,525 | 0.683 | + 10,709 |
| 5 | + 15,680 | 0.681 | + 10,678 | 0.621 | + 9,737 |
| 6 | + 15,680 | 0.630 | + 9,878 | 0.564 | + 8,844 |
| 7 | + 15,680 | 0.583 | + 9,141 | 0.513 | + 8,044 |
| 8 | + 15,680 | 0.540 | + 8,467 | 0.467 | + 7,323 |
| 9 | + 15,680 | 0.500 | + 7,840 | 0.424 | + 6,648 |
| 10 | + 15,680 | 0.463 | + 7,260 | 0.386 | + 6,052 |
| | + 56,100 | | + 4,497 | | - 4,362 |

Project has a positive NPV @ 8%, will generate surplus and should be accepted. If the cost of capital rises to 10%, project moves into deficit. The project is therefore marginal and highly risky on present assumptions.

# Vale Park Golf Driving Range

## d) Cash Flow Forecast Revenue Estimates next financial year

| | MAR | APL | MAY | JUN | JUL | AUG | SEP | OCT | NOV | DEC | JAN | FEB | MAR | TOTAL |
|---|---|---|---|---|---|---|---|---|---|---|---|---|---|---|
| No. of weeks taken | | 5 | 4 | 4 | 5 | 4 | 4 | 5 | 4 | 3 | 5 | 4 | 4 | 51 |
| | | £ | £ | £ | £ | £ | £ | £ | £ | £ | £ | £ | £ | £ |
| RECEIPTS | | 4,000 | 3,200 | 4,400 | 5,500 | 4,400 | 4,400 | 4,000 | 1,800 | 1,350 | 2,250 | 1,800 | 3,200 | 40,300 |
| PAYMENTS | | | | | | | | | | | | | | |
| Maintenance £60 p.w. | | 300 | 240 | 240 | 300 | 240 | 240 | 300 | 240 | 240 | 300 | 240 | 240 | 3,120 |
| Advertising | | 125 | 125 | 125 | 125 | 125 | 125 | 125 | 125 | 125 | 125 | 125 | 125 | 1,500 |
| Staff | | 1,667 | 1,667 | 1,666 | 1,667 | 1,667 | 1,666 | 1,667 | 1,667 | 1,666 | 1,667 | 1,667 | 1,666 | 20,000 |
| Set-up costs: Nets | | 2,200 | | | | | | | | | | | | 2,200 |
| Golf Clubs | | 3,000 | | | | | | | | | | | | 3,000 |
| Marketing | | 500 | | | | | | | | | | | | 500 |
| | | 7,792 | 2,032 | 2,031 | 2,092 | 2,032 | 2,031 | 2,092 | 2,032 | 2,031 | 2,092 | 2,032 | 2,031 | 30,320 |
| bal. b/f | | - | -3,792 | -2,624 | -255 | 3,153 | 5,521 | 7,890 | 9,798 | 9,566 | 8,885 | 9,043 | 8,811 | |
| bal. c/f | | -3,792 | -2,624 | -255 | 3,153 | 5,521 | 7,890 | 9,798 | 9,566 | 8,885 | 9,043 | 8,811 | 9,980 | |

## e) Recovery Rates Forecast on Revenue Estimates

Year 1 only    $\dfrac{\text{Estimated Revenue}}{\text{Estimated Expenditure}} \dfrac{40,300}{30,320} \times 100\% = \underline{133\%}$

Year 2 onwards    $\dfrac{\text{Estimated Revenue}}{\text{Estimated Expenditure}} \dfrac{40,300}{24,620} \times 100\% = \underline{164\%}$

## f) Key Points for Operational Control

### Physical
Controls over cash - use of a till, regular bankings, safe deposit etc.
Controls over assets - counting golf clubs, locking them up overnight, issuing receipts for return after hire etc.
Checking condition of nets so balls do not get lost.

### Financial
Reconciliation of cash takings.
Keeping forecasts up to date and using budget to monitor and control results
Paying bills on time, but not early.
Putting surplus cash on deposit.
Wages checks.    etc.

## Vale Park Golf Driving Range

g) A contractor bidding to manage the Driving Range would bid for a comparatively short term (commonly four years) and would not be concerned with the capital investment decision and the need to recoup initial capital outlays. The contractor's performance will be measured by a comparison of actual recovery rate(s) with target recovery rate(s), based on annual operating results. (In contrast, the local authority will seek to ensure that the project is viable over its whole life. This project has a payback period of under 7 years, with a life of 10 years, and it also meets the criterion of a positive NPV at 8% cost of capital.)

If the terms of the contract so specify, the contractor may be responsible for replacement of equipment and may also be entitled to an element of profit-sharing or income-sharing. The presence of either or both of these factors will result in the contractor aiming to generate a surplus. (In contrast, the local authority will not be seeking to build up a surplus in any one year at the expense of current council tax payers and will be conscious of the need for political accountability to tax payers year on year.)

A contractor free to set prices will want the flexibility to alter prices and re-negotiate costs throughout the period of the contract as conditions change. (In contrast, the local authority budget process is more rigid and the Estimates as approved by the Finance Committee and subsequently published will generally be expected to stand without alteration.)

Any manager of the Driving Range, whether a local authority employee or a contractor, will be concerned with systems for good cash control and with accurate, adequate and timely management and accounting information.

## Salhaven Watersports Centre

a) **Recovery Rates**

Latest year (Year 1) (using projected outturn figures)

$$\frac{\text{Total Revenue}}{\text{Total Expenditure}} \times 100\% \quad \frac{£103,800^*}{£224,000} \times 100\% = \mathbf{46\%} \text{ Target revenue}$$

$$\begin{array}{ll}
\text{Year 2} \times \dfrac{103}{100} & £106,914 \\[2mm]
\text{Year 3} \times \dfrac{103^2}{100} & £110,121 \\[2mm]
\text{Year 4} \times \dfrac{103^3}{100} & £113,425
\end{array}$$

\* applying maximum permitted price increase

Final year (Year 4) (using projected revenue targets) to achieve a 50% recovery rate

$$\frac{\text{Total Revenue}}{\text{Total Expenditure}} \times 100\% \quad \frac{113,425}{x} \times 100\% = \mathbf{50\%}$$

Therefore Total Expenditure must be **£226,850** or less by Year 4.

This sets the framework for the operating budgets throughout the period of the contract. With the limits set on revenue, the manager will have to find ways to hold back the expenditure to £226,850 by Year 4 from the current level of £224,000. The limit on annual gross expenditure is not a constraining factor here because the recovery rate target and revenue targets set the effective limits for this contract; however if either of these two effective constraints were removed, the third constraint might become important.

b) **Notes** | **Revenue Budget next financial year**

| | Latest Outturn | £ |
|---|---|---|
| | 17 weeks @ £ 800 pw = | 13,600 |
| | 18 weeks @ £3,100 pw = | 55,800 |
| | 17 weeks @ £1,200 pw = | 20,400 |
| | 52 | 89,800 |
| | of which schools | 25,000 |
| | clubs | 3,600 |
| | casual users (balance) | 61,200 |
| | | 89,800 |
| | Catering | 14,000 |
| 1 | TOTAL REVENUE | 103,800 |

| | Next Year's Target | | £ |
|---|---|---|---|
| | applying maximum 3% increase | $\times \dfrac{103}{100}$ | |
| | equally to all users | | |
| | schools | | 25,750 |
| | clubs | | 3,708 |
| | casual | | 63,036 |
| | | | 92,494 |
| | | | 92,494 |
| | Catering | $\times \dfrac{103}{100}$ | 14,420 |
| | TOTAL REVENUE | | 106,914 |

# Salhaven Watersports Centre

| Notes | | Latest Outturn £ | Changes | Next Year's Budget (Year 2) £ |
|---|---|---|---|---|
| 2 | **Expenditure Budget next financial year** | | | |
| | **Staff Costs** | | | |
| | Salaries, wages, NI | 100,000 | + 2% | 102,000 |
| | Uniforms, wet suits etc | 1,000 | none | 1,000 |
| | Training | 2,000 | none | 2,000 |
| | | 103,000 | | 105,000 |
| | **Centre Operating Costs** | | | |
| | Energy costs | 30,000 | + 5% | 31,500 |
| | Equipment | 35,000 | − £3,500 | 31,500 |
| | Insurances | 10,000 | + 10% | 11,000 |
| | Office | 6,000 | none | 6,000 |
| | Provisions bar & catering | 12,000 | none | 12,000 |
| | Repairs and maintenance | 8,000 | none | 8,000 |
| | | 101,000 | | 100,000 |
| | **Central Services Costs** | | | |
| | Finance | 3,000 | | |
| | Legal | 500 | | |
| | Management & admin | 9,000 | | |
| | Marketing | 7,500 | | |
| | | 20,000 | none | 20,000 |
| | **TOTAL GROSS EXPENDITURE** | 224,000 | | 225,000 |

A target of £225,000 gross expenditure for next year (Year 2 of contract) will give

$$\text{Recovery Rate} \quad \frac{£106,914}{£225,000} \times 100\% = 47.5\%$$

## Notes

1 The major assumption underlying the preparation of operating budgets for the Centre is that activity levels remain unchanged from year to year. Price increases have been applied to the same activity levels. If the activity levels can be increased, more revenue can be generated, allowing expenditure levels to rise as well within the overall limits imposed by the recovery rate target.

## Salhaven Watersports Centre

### Notes

2  Following on from the assumption of unchanged activity levels, an expenditure budget has been set which is designed to improve the recovery rate for next year bringing it closer towards the target for Year 4. Uncontrollable items (Central Services Costs) and known unavoidable increases (Salaries, Energy, Insurances) have been estimated first. Other budgets have been left at latest year levels rather than cut back and the burden of the reduced overall target has been borne by the Equipment budget which is a controllable budget. [Other possibilities exist, including cutbacks to all controllable budgets or to a different combination of budget heads.] The budget shown above shows a target recovery rate of 47.5%; an improvement on latest year performance and a step towards the Year 4 target. Larger increases in the recovery rate target can be achieved next year by cutting expenditure budgets further.

If bar and catering figures are excluded, in line with Audit Commission (1983) guidelines, the recovery rates are:

|  | Latest year (Year 1) | Next year (Year 2) | Year 3† | Year 4# |
|---|---|---|---|---|
| $\dfrac{\text{Total Revenue}}{\text{Total Expenditure}} \times 100\%$ | $\dfrac{89,800}{212,000}$ | $\dfrac{92,494}{213,000}$ | $\dfrac{95,269}{214,000}$ | $\dfrac{98,127}{214,850}$ |
|  | **42%** | **43%** | **45%** | **46%** |

†   Revenue target £110,121 less catering £14,000 $\frac{103}{100}$ [2]

    Expenditure target guestimate: overall 0.5% increase on preceding year.

\#   Revenue target £113,425 less catering £14,000 $\frac{103}{100}$ [3]

    Expenditure target guestimate: Year 4 target above £226,850 less £12,000 catering expenditure.

This shows that the surplus on bar and catering is crucial to the achievement of the target recovery rate.

# Salhaven Watersports Centre

Notes

### Windsurfing Proposal

|  | £ |
|---|---|
| Estimated revenue from one session | 40 |
| Variable costs (staff) 3 hours @ £8 per hour | 24 |
| CONTRIBUTION FROM ONE SESSION | 16 |

With two sessions programmed each week the windsurfing activity will contribute; 52 weeks x 2 sessions x £16 contribution per session = £1,664.

Against this must be offset the cost of the equipment. The equipment has an expected life of five years but in order to meet the Centre manager's financial (short-term) target of break-even within two years, the cost needs to be allocated to the first two years (Years 2 and 3 of the contract).

| | | Year 2 | Year 3 | Year 4 |
|---|---|---|---|---|
| | | £ | £ | £ |
| 3 | Revenue from windsurfing each year | 4,160 | 4,284 | 4,413 |
| 4 | Variable costs (staff) | (2,496) | (2,545) | (2,596) |
| | Contribution | 1,664 | 1,739 | 1,817 |
| | Cost of equipment allocated | (1,500) | (1,500) | (-) |
| | Estimated surplus | 164 | 239 | 1,817 |
| | Expected Recovery Rate $\frac{\text{Estimated Revenue}}{\text{Estimated Expenditure}}$ x 100% | $\frac{4,160}{3,996}$ | $\frac{4,284}{4,045}$ | $\frac{4,413}{2,596}$ |
| | | 104% | 105% | 170% |

On the basis of the estimates provided, the proposal for windsurfing meets both the targets: that of the Centre manager for break-even within two years and that of the Centre for a recovery rate of 50% by the end of the contract.

Other factors would be considered, including the uncertainties surrounding the cost estimates; any additional marketing costs needed in addition to the marketing budget already contained in the service level agreement; uncertainties of customer demand; uncertainties of weather conditions before a final decision is taken.

### Notes

3 The maximum permitted 3% increase has been applied to revenue estimates.

4 Staff costs have been increased at 2% per year compound in line with next year's operating budget assumptions.

# Oxley Sports and Social Club

a) Budgeted Profit and Loss Account for next year

| | £ | |
|---|---:|---|
| Turnover | 1,720,400 | latest year + 10% |
| Other operating income | 250,000 | no change |
| | 1,970,400 | |
| | | |
| Staff costs | 939,360 | latest year + 3% |
| Depreciation | 131,000 | no change |
| Other operating costs | 654,480 | latest year + 8% |
| | 1,724,840 | |
| Operating profit | 245,560 | |
| Interest payable | 76,500 | latest year - 10% |
| Profit for the year | 169,060 | |
| Balance at 1st April latest | (150,000) | |
| Balance at 31st March next | 19,060 | |

Budgeted Balance Sheet next year

| | £ | |
|---|---:|---|
| Fixed Assets | | |
| Land and buildings (at cost) | 1,093,000 | latest value £556,000 less next year's depreciation £131,000 |
| Equipment and Fixtures (net) | 425,000 | |
| | 1,518,000 | |
| Current Assets: Stock | 33,000 | latest stock turnover ratio 30÷1,564x365 days = 7 days. £1,720,400÷365x7 days = next year's closing stock. |
| Debtors | 60,500 | latest debtors collection 55÷1,564x365 days = 12.8 days. £1,720,400÷365x12.8 days = next year's closing debtors. |
| Cash (see Working) | 132,660 | |
| | 226,160 | |
| | | |
| Creditors: amounts falling due within one year (1) | 217,100 | |
| Net current assets | 9,060 | |
| Total assets less current liabilities | 1,527,060 | |
| Creditors: amounts falling due after more than one year (2) | 902,000 | |
| | 625,060 | |
| | | |
| Capital and reserves | | |
| Capital fund: | | |
| Balance at 1st April latest | 586,000 | no change |
| Profit and loss account | 19,060 | from budgeted profit and loss account |
| | 605,060 | |
| Repairs and renewals fund | 20,000 | no change |
| | 625,060 | |

# Oxley Sports and Social Club

(1)  Creditors
| | £ | |
|---|---|---|
| Overdraft | - | see Working |
| Trade creditors | 85,800 | latest creditors payment period 78÷1,564x 365 days = 18.2 days.  £1,720,400÷365x18.2 days = next year's closing creditors. |
| Social security and other taxes | 40,000 | no change |
| Other creditors | 91,300 | latest creditors payment period 83÷1,564x 365 days = 19.4 days.  £1,720,400÷365x 19.4 days = next year's closing creditors. |
| | 217,100 | |

(2)  Creditors
| | £ | |
|---|---|---|
| Bank Loan | 680,000 | as given |
| Loan from Oxley Council | 222,000 | as given |
| | 902,000 | |

## Cash Working

| | £ | | | £ |
|---|---|---|---|---|
| Opening cash balance (latest balance sheet) | 44,000 | | Opening overdraft | 171,000 |
| **Cash Receipts** | | | **Cash Payments** | |
| Operating cash surplus | 300,060 | | Change in stocks | 3,000 |
| Change in creditors | 16,100 | | Change in debtors | 5,500 |
| | | | Loans repaid | 48,000 |
| | | | CLOSING CASH (balancing figure) | 132,660 |
| | 360,160 | | | 360,160 |

**Cash Receipts**

Operating cash surplus = Profit for year + depreciation
£300,060          £169,060          £131,000

Change in creditors = opening creditors - closing creditors
£16,100     (£78,000 + £40,000 + £83,000)     (£85,800 + £40,000 + £91,300)

**Cash Payments**

Change in stocks = opening stock - closing stock
£3,000          £30,000          £33,000

Change in debtors = opening debtors - closing debtors
£5,500          £55,000          £60,500

Loans repaid = opening loans - closing loans
£950,000          £902,000

- 40 -

## Oxley Sports and Social Club

b)

### Key Points for Financial Control

In order to achieve the relatively ambitious target set for next year, the Secretary will need to concentrate on two major areas - control of operating costs as business increases and control of working capital. This will lead to the generation of cash needed firstly to pay off the overdraft and secondly to re-build positive cash balances.

**Control of operating costs:** an increase in membership and in usage could lead to a demand from members for more/better facilities which will inevitably increase the costs. The case study tells us that a major refurbishment is only 2 or 3 years old so the Secretary should be able to resist such demands in the short term. A possible area of difficulty could be in the staff costs budget where the projected increase of 3% makes it hard to recruit more staff within budget; the Secretary could look at working practices to ensure that staff are employed on terms which give sufficient flexibility to cover peak demand periods. The new marketing budget should be monitored closely to ensure that value for money is obtained from the expenditure; new members can be asked how they heard about the Club, advertising responses can be collected, user surveys can be carried out. With newly refurbished premises, day to day repairs and maintenance should be relatively low giving scope for close control over this budget.

**Control of working capital:** every item can be monitored frequently and regularly against budget with action taken to halt a trend of overspending if discovered. Stock will include bar, catering and consumable items, each probably the responsibility of a different member of staff who will need to control stocks by means of stock counts (one-off or continuous), reconciliations between physical quantities and monetary amounts shown in the accounts, checks for obsolete/slow-moving items, physical security of stocks, appropriate authorisation for placing orders, legal requirements where applicable and use of internal audit or professional stock valuers from time to time.

The balance sheets show amounts for debtors indicating that the Club does offer credit terms to users. Controls could include checking the creditworthiness of a customer before granting credit, issuing invoices promptly and chasing late payments vigorously and efficiently.

The Club receives credit terms from suppliers and should take the maximum period of credit offered to conserve its cash as well as reviewing the credit terms and re-negotiating a more advantageous credit period if possible.

LEEDS METROPOLITAN
UNIVERSITY LIBRARY

## Oxley Sports and Social Club

Cash balances (and overdraft) are controlled by having a cash flow forecast, keeping it up-to-date and using that information to anticipate times of cash surplus when balances can be moved into interest-bearing deposit accounts and times of cash deficit which can be minimised. Most banks offer special accounts for charities where interest is paid without deduction of income tax.

Regular management information will include reports of factual against £budget for each budget head and variances in £ and as % of budget.

For stocks:     stock turnover ratio and lists of physical stock count items with £value
                                (at least annually, preferably quarterly)
                                (monthly)

For debtors:    debtors collection period and aged debtors listing
                                (monthly)

For creditors:  creditors payment period and creditors listing
                                (monthly)

For cash:       cash flow forecast updated with factual and bank reconciliation statement
                                (weekly)
                                (monthly)

**Bogood Breweries**

a)

| Comparative ratios | | Notes | Industry | Bogood (latest) | Bogood (previous) |
|---|---|---|---|---|---|
| **Liquidity** | | | | | |
| Short-term: | Acid test | (1) | 0.9 : 1 | $\frac{748}{839}$ 0.89 : 1 | $\frac{785}{762}$ 1.03 : 1 |
| | Current | (2) | n/a | $\frac{903}{839}$ 1.07 : 1 | $\frac{991}{762}$ 1.30 : 1 |
| | Debtor's collection | | n/a | $\frac{276 \times 365}{2,842}$ 35 days | $\frac{251 \times 365}{2,305}$ 39 days |
| Longer-term: | Gearing | (3) | 75% | $\frac{1,659}{1,965}$ 84% | $\frac{1,446}{1,829}$ 79% |
| | Interest cover | | 7 | $\frac{341}{76}$ 4.5 | $\frac{270}{49}$ 5.5 |
| **Profitability** | | | | | |
| Return on net assets | | | 7.5% | $\frac{341}{3,115}$ 10.9% | $\frac{270}{2,829}$ 9.5% |
| Net asset turnover | | | 0.75 times | $\frac{2,842}{3,115}$ 0.9 times | $\frac{2,305}{2,829}$ 0.8 times |
| Return on sales | | | 10% | $\frac{341}{2,842}$ 12.0% | $\frac{270}{2,305}$ 11.7% |
| **Shareholders' measures** | | | | | |
| Dividend cover | | | 50% | $\frac{39}{175}$ 22% | $\frac{36}{149}$ 24% |
| Dividend yield | | | 6% | $\frac{6.5 \text{ pence}}{182 \text{ pence}}$ 3.6% | n/a |
| Earnings per share (EPS) | | | 35 pence | $\frac{175}{600}$ 29.17pence | $\frac{149}{600}$ 24.83 pence |
| Price Earnings ratio (P/E) | | | 6.3 | $\frac{182 \text{ pence}}{29.17 \text{ pence}}$ 6.24 | n/a |

**Notes**

(1) Acid test ratio assumes conversion into cash in a time period of a week or two:-

Current assets included: Cash £80,000 + Investment at market value £392,000 + Debtors £276,000 = £748,000 [Latest Year]

Current liabilities included: Overdraft (unsecured) £509,000 + Trade creditors £330,000 = £839,000 [Latest Year]

# Bogood Breweries

## Notes

(2) Current ratio assumes conversion into cash in a period of between four and six weeks:-

Current assets included: Total as for acid test ratio £748,000 + Stock £155,000 = [Latest Year] £903,000

Current liabilities included: Total as for acid test ratio £839,000 [Latest Year]

(3) To provide a comparison with the industry average method of calculation

Total loans [Latest Year]: Debenture 2005 £1,000,000 + Bank Loan £150,000 + Overdraft £509,000 = £1,659,000

Shareholders' funds: Called up share capital £600,000 + Revaluation reserve [Latest Year] £785,000 + Profit and loss account £580,000 = £1,965,000

b) The liquidity ratios for Bogood show that the company is in a weaker position than the industry average; gearing is higher than average and the latest year figure shows an increase on that of the previous year an unwelcome trend for a company seeking to expand by means of further borrowing. The interest cover shows the company to be much more vulnerable to interest rate rises than the industry average. The acid test ratio is comparable with the industry average but worsening from the previous year to the latest year. The current ratio shows the same trend and highlights a need for management action before the company becomes insolvent. A slight improvement in the average period for outstanding debts may be an indication that action to control working capital is being taken.

Profitability has increased from previous to latest year and is above the industry average. Both higher profit margins and a faster asset turnover have been achieved and have contributed to an overall return on net assets increase.

The shareholders can see a higher EPS for the latest year which reflects the increasing profitability of their company, but high gearing is keeping the dividend cover and dividend yield lower than industry averages. The share price seems to have become adjusted to reflect this situation because the P/E ratio is close to the industry average.

**Bogood Breweries**

c)

| A Year | B C/F | C Tax on C/F 30% x B | D Tax Allowance 25% WDA | E Tax Saved 30% x allowance | F Tax Paid (C - E) | G C/F after tax (B - F) | PV @ 12% | |
|---|---|---|---|---|---|---|---|---|
| 0 | -500,000 | | 125,000 (1) | 37,500 | +37,500 saved | -462,500 | 1.000 | -462,500 |
| 1 | +150,000 | | 93,750 | 28,125 | +28,125 saved | +178,125 | 0.893 | +159,066 |
| 2 | +150,000 | 45,000 | 70,312 | 21,094 | -23,906 | +126,094 | 0.797 | +100,497 |
| 3 | +150,000 | 45,000 | 52,735 | 15,820 | -29,180 | +120,820 | 0.712 | +86,024 |
| 4 | +150,000 | 45,000 | 39,500 | 11,865 | -33,135 | +116,865 | 0.636 | +74,326 |
| 5 | +150,000 | 45,000 | 118,653 (2) | 35,596 | -9,404 | +140,596 | 0.567 | +79,718 |
| 6 | - | 45,000 | - | - | -45,000 | -45,000 | 0.507 | -22,815 |
| NPVs | +250,000 | | | | | | | +14,316 |

Notes

(1) Tax allowances have been taken immediately on the <u>assumption</u> that the company has sufficient profits from its existing business against which these allowances can be offset. Were this not to be the case, tax allowances would be received only against profits generated by this project, thus delaying the receipt of allowances until later in the life of the project, which would affect the cash flows after tax and the resulting NPVs.

(2) The balance of remaining tax allowances is received at the end of the project (end of Year 5).

d) The bank manager is concerned primarily with Bogood's solvency and with the management of working capital. As detailed in (b), the solvency of the company shows a worsening trend and gearing is comparatively high.

The new investment shows a low expected net present value at the company's discount rate of 12% and it should be noted that the initial loan interest rate is 12.5% and could rise. Before lending Bogood the £500,000 the bank could ask for a re-appraisal of the project's cash flows as well as evidence that the directors are improving the day-to-day control of working capital. The bank might insist that Bogood uses its short term deposits towards paying off some of its overdraft, and that the company's declared policy of future dividends growth is reviewed, in order to conserve cash.

# Abbey Farm Forest

a) Budgeted Income and Expenditure Account for the first year of the Recreation and Sport Programme

| Notes | Income | £ | £ |
|---|---|---|---|
| | **Income** | | |
| | From Motorcycle Rally Clubs: | | |
| | Membership: 80 families @ £25 | 2,000 | |
| 1 | Open use weekends: 30 riders x 20 weekends @ £5 | 3,000 | |
| 2 | Event weekends:[average number of competitors 247.5 @ £2 + club fee £200] x 4 weekends | 2,780 | 7,780 |
| | From Horse Riding Clubs: 20 Clubs @ £100 | | 2,000 |
| | From Shooting Clubs: Membership: 100 @ £50 | | 5,000 |
| | From Corporate Hospitality: | | |
| 3 | Average number of competitors 45 @ £20 x 60 days | | 54,000 |
| | TOTAL INCOME | | 68,780 |
| | **Expenditure** | | |
| | Maintenance and staffing for Forest: 52 weeks @ £100 | 5,200 | |
| 4 | Commission to agent for Corporate Hospitality management | 40,500 | |
| 5 | Depreciation | 7,400 | (53,100) |
| | Net Profit before owners' salaries and taxation | | 15,680 |

Budgeted Balance Sheet as at the close of the first year

| Notes | | £ | £ |
|---|---|---|---|
| 6 | **Fixed Assets** | | |
| | Tangible assets | | 99,600 |
| 7 | **Current Assets** | | |
| | Cash in hand | | 23,080 |
| | Total Assets Less Current Liabilities | | 122,680 |
| 8 | **Capital and Reserves** | | |
| | Owners' opening capital | 107,000 | |
| | Net Profit | 15,680 | |
| | | | 122,680 |

- 46 -

## Abbey Farm Forest

The budget for the first year of the recreation and sport programme shows that the Wrights are likely to achieve their profit target, provided that their estimates of income and expenditure are reasonably accurate; or, if not, that they are able during the year to respond to changed conditions either by attracting more users, increasing prices, reducing costs or a combination of these actions.

When the budget is measured against the profit target, it shows

|  | Profit target | Income target | Expenditure target |
|---|---|---|---|
| Margins of safety | £(15,680 - 12,000)<br>£15,680 | £(68,780 - 65,100)<br>£68,780 | £(53,100 - 56,780)<br>£53,100 |
|  | 23%↓ | 5.3%↓ | 6.9%↑ |

Profit can decrease by 23%, or Income can decrease by 5.3%, of Expenditure can increase by 6.9% before the target is not met. This shows that the Income target is the most sensitive to changes in expectations and the Wrights would be advised to monitor income received against budget most closely.

## Abbey Farm Forest

b) **Performance Measurement of the Recreation and Sport Programme**

Notes | **Activity measures**

Each of the assumptions made in the preparation of the budget will need to be tested against actual outcome.

|  | Estimate | Actual | +/- | % difference |
|---|---|---|---|---|
| **INCOME** | | | | |
| Motorcycle Rally Clubs | | | | |
| Number of family memberships | 80 | | | |
| Number of open use weekends | 20 | | | |
| Number of riders at each open use weekend: dates | 30 | | | |
|  | 30 | | | |
|  | 30 | | | |
| etc | | | | |
| Number of event weekends | 4 | | | |
| Number of riders at event weekends: dates | 247.5 | | | |
|  | 247.5 | | | |
| etc | 247.5 | | | |
| Horse Riding Clubs | | | | |
| Number of participating clubs | 20 | | | |
| Number of weekends access permitted | 24 | | | |
| Shooting Clubs | | | | |
| Number of memberships | 100 | | | |
| Number of days access permitted | 60 | | | |
| Corporate Hospitality | | | | |
| Number of days access permitted | 60 | | | |
| Number of competitors at each day: dates | 45 | | | |
|  | 45 | | | |
|  | 45 | | | |
| **EXPENDITURE** | | | | |
| Number of weeks extra staffing | 52 | | | |

9

- 48 -

## Abbey Farm Forest

### Notes

### Budgetary control

Each of the income and expenditure budgets will need to be compared with actual and a budget variance computed. This is commonly done on a monthly basis.

| 10 | MONTH OF ............. | Budget Estimate | Actual | Variance from Budget over/under | % difference |
|---|---|---|---|---|---|
| | | £ | £ | £ | £ |
| INCOME | | | | | |
| Motorcycle Rally Clubs: | | | | | |
| Membership | | | | | |
| Open use weekends | | | | | |
| Event weekends | | | | | |
| Horse Riding Clubs: | | | | | |
| Membership | | | | | |
| Shooting Clubs: | | | | | |
| Membership | | | | | |
| Corporate Hospitality: | | | | | |
| Competitors | | | | | |
| EXPENDITURE | | | | | |
| Maintenance and staffing | | | | | |
| Commission to agent | | | | | |
| Depreciation | | | | | |
| PROFIT/(LOSS) | | | | | |

### Ratio Analysis

### Activity

Various activity measures could be used. A suitable example is $\dfrac{\text{Actual Activity}}{\text{Budgeted Activity}} \times 100\%$

Expressed in this way, a 100% measure indicates that activity is exactly as budgeted, a percentage greater than 100% indicates greater activity and a percentage lower than 100% less activity than budgeted.

# Abbey Farm Forest

## Revenue variances

To link activity with revenue

Price variance            Actual activity level x [Budget price - Actual price]
Activity Volume variance   Budget price x [Actual activity level - Budget activity level]

eg A corporate hospitality day on 4th May

CLIENT ..................    DATE   4th May

| | Budget Estimate £ | Actual £ | Variance £ |
|---|---|---|---|
| | 900 | 950 | 50* over budget |

```
45 competitors @ £20 per person
50 competitors
Price Variance  50 x £(20 - 950/50)  = £ 50   under-budget
                £20 x (50 - 45)       = £100   over-budget
                              NET       £ 50*  over-budget
```

On this date, more people attended than were expected, but the average charge was less than the budget estimate. This helps to focus managers' attention on the causes of the variance which might otherwise be obscured in the routine budgetary control reports.

The fact that this particular variance is favourable (more income was received than budgeted for) might tempt managers to ignore it and not look closely, but there are insights to be gained which can help to determine future pricing and marketing policies.

## Liquidity

Cash flow will need to be monitored closely and cash balances reviewed monthly at least.

If credit terms are offered to any of the proposed users then a debtors' collection period measure will be needed.

## Abbey Farm Forest

### Investment

The Wrights are financing Abbey Farm Forest out of savings and need a measure that can be compared against alternative uses for their cash.

Return on net assets is suitable here:

Using the first year's budget figures:

| | | |
|---|---|---|
| Profit before owners' salaries and taxation | £15,680 | 29% |
| Average investment £107,000 ÷ 2 | £53,500 | |
| Profit before owners' salaries and taxation | £15,680 | 14.6% |
| Initial investment | £107,000 | |
| Profit after owners' salaries and before taxation | £3,680 | 6.8% |
| Average investment | £53,500 | |

### Notes

1  Assuming the most pessimistic estimate of use.

2  Average usage has been chosen on the basis of expected value (EV) computed by multiplying each estimate by its expected probability and adding the results:
EV (number of riders) = (350x0.05) + (300x0.25) + (250x0.35) + (200x0.30) + (150x0.05)
= 247.5

EV is an arithmetic result which does not itself represent a precise estimate of outcome (0.5 of a rider is meaningless!) but enables preparation of a budget when outcomes are uncertain.

3  EV (number of competitors) = (60x0.05) + (55x0.1) + (50x0.2) + (45x0.3) + (40x0.2) + (35x0.1) + (30x0.05) = 45

Here, because of the particular distribution of estimate, the EV is also the "mean" and the "mode". Budget-preparers choose from EV, mean and mode when compiling estimates.

4  75% commission x budgeted income £54,000.

5  Under the historical cost accounting convention land is not normally depreciated. Depreciation has been provided on the fencing, signs and vehicle cost on a straight line basis over five years.

## Abbey Farm Forest

6    Tangible assets valued at cost less depreciation provided.

7    Initial investment £107,000 + cash received from operations £68,780 minus cost of tangible assets £107,000 + cash expenses £(5,200 + 40,500) = £23,080 cash balance.

8    Owners' initial investment in land £70,000 + fencing £15,000 + signs £2,000 + vehicle £20,000 = £107,000.

9    The assumption throughout is that spectators are not charged for entrance to the Forest.

10   One of the major problem areas in budget-setting is the split of an annual figure over the individual months. When seasonal differences can be estimated reliably then the budget is often split on this basis; otherwise a "rule of thumb" method is used such as splitting the annual allocation 1/12 to each month.

     Care needs to be taken in interpreting MONTHLY variances when the budget is in operational terms an ANNUAL one.

c)   Key Points for Operational Control

### Physical

Controls over cash-use of a till for receipts, regular bankings, safe deposit. The size of the Forest and the cost of staff required to collect fees may suggest the use of an "honesty box" system whereby a user pays for a ticket on entry to the Forest. Rangers then check tickets on an ad-hoc basis and have the power to fine anyone found to be participating without a ticket. Controls over assets-checking condition of fencing, signposting, paths etc to ensure safety for users and security. Compliance with health and safety regulations for users and staff.

### Financial

Reconciliation of cash takings. Putting surplus cash on deposit. Keeping forecasts up to date and using the budget to monitor and control results. Putting surplus cash on deposit. Responding quickly to price and activity variances by changing prices and/or targeting marketing efforts. The largest component of income being from Corporate Hospitality it is worth extra management effort to ensure this source of income continues.

# Topflight

a) i) Total cost function (TC)

Annual fixed cost (FC) = Servicing £45,000 + Crew £90,000 + Depreciation of airship £(1,200,000 ÷ 5 years) - Advertising revenue £25,000 = Net £350,000

Variable cost per passenger (VC) = £25

TC = FC + VCx; where x represents the number of passengers a year

**TC = £350,000 + £25x**

Total revenue function (TR)

Demand schedule based on market research limits of prices of £300 (upper) and £120 (lower):

| Price per passenger £ | Passenger demand | TR £ | |
|---|---|---|---|
| 300 | 0 | 0 | At £300, demand is zero. |
| 280 | 500 | 140,000 | Demand increases by 500 |
| 260 | 1,000 | 260,000 | passengers for each £20 |
| 240 | 1,500 | 360,000 | decrease in price a |
| 220 | 2,000 | 440,000 | relationship of £20 |
| 200 | 2,500 | 500,000 | 500 |
| 180 | 3,000 | 540,000 | passengers or 4 pence |
| 160 | 3,500 | 560,000 | per passenger |
| 140 | 4,000 | 560,000 | |
| 120 | 4,500 | 540,000 | |

Maximum selling price for one passenger is represented by SP = £300 - £0.04x

TR = SPx; where x represents the number of passengers a year

TR = (£300 - £0.04x)x

**TR = £300x - £0.04x$^2$**

# Topflight

## a) ii) Pricing decision

[Note: other methods including graphical analysis can be used to determine optimal selling price which coincides with the activity level at which the highest profit is expected.]

Arithmetically, optimal price is found using simple differential calculus to equate the marginal cost (MC) with the marginal revenue (MR):

$$TC = £350,000 + £25x$$
$$MC = \frac{dTC}{dx}$$
$$MC = £25 \quad (1)$$

$$TR = £300x - £0.04x^2$$
$$MR = \frac{dTR}{dx}$$
$$MR = £300 - £0.08x \quad (2)$$

At the optimal activity level $MC = MR$
Substituting (1) and (2)    $£25 = £300 - £0.08x$
Solving for x gives    $x = 3,437.5$
The price at this activity level $SP = £300 - £0.04(3,437.5)$ gives a unit price of **£162.50**

## iii) Flexible budgets

|  | Activity level (number of passengers a year) | | | | |
|---|---|---|---|---|---|
|  | 2,500 | 3,000 | 3,438 (rounded) | 3,500 | 4,000 |
|  | £ | £ | £ | £ | £ |
| Sales revenue | (@ £200) 500,000 | (@ £180) 540,000 | (@ 162.50) 558,675 | (@ £160) 560,000 | (@ £140) 560,000 |
| Less: variable costs | (@£25) 62,500 | 75,000 | 85,950 | 87,500 | 100,000 |
| Contribution | 437,500 | 465,000 | 472,725 | 472,500 | 460,000 |
| Less: fixed costs | 350,000 | 350,000 | 350,000 | 350,000 | 350,000 |
| Profit | 87,500 | 115,000 | 122,725 | 122,500 | 110,000 |

A price charged of £162.50 per passenger is expected to generate an annual passenger demand of 3,438 which will produce a maximum profit level of £122,725.

# Topflight

## b) Capacity utilisation

Based on market research estimated probabilities:

Expected value [EV] of number of passengers per flight
[20x0.05]+[19x0.05]+[18x0.10]+[17x0.10]+[16x0.20]+[15x0.15]+[13x0.15]+[11x0.10]+[10x0.10] = **14.95** passengers per flight

Using EV:

Annual demand (see (a)) 3,437.5 passengers ÷ EV per flight 14.95 = **230 flights per year**

OR

Using the most likely estimate of passenger numbers (80% has the highest individual probability)

Annual demand 3,437.5 passengers ÷ most likely estimate 16.00 = **215 flights per year**

The use of market research estimates in these two different, but equally valid, ways gives the estimated number of flights per year as 215 or 230. For the first year, the management of Glenhall may decide to be cautious and book only 215 flights risking a slightly lower level of profit than should be obtained from catering for all levels of demand by booking 230 flights.

## c)

i) Annual depreciation charge = $\dfrac{\text{£Initial Outlay} - \text{£Scrap Value}}{\text{Estimated useful life of asset}}$ = $\dfrac{\text{£1,200,000} - \text{£NIL}}{5 \text{ years}}$ = £240,000

using straight-line basis

| Return on Investment | Notes | Year 1 | Year 2 | Year 3 | Year 4 | Year 5 | Overall |
|---|---|---|---|---|---|---|---|
| Profit x 100% | (1) | 122,587 | 122,587 | 122,587 | 122,587 | 122,587 | 122,587 |
| Average Investment | (2) | £(1.2m+0.96m)÷2 | £(0.96m+0.72m)÷2 | £(0.72m+0.48m)÷2 | £(0.48m+0.24m)÷2 | £(0.24m-NIL)÷2 | 600,000 |
| | | 122,587 | 122,587 | 122,587 | 122,587 | 122,587 | |
| | | 1,080,000 | 840,000 | 600,000 | 360,000 | 120,000 | |
| | (3) | 11.3% | 14.6% | 20.4% | 34.1% | 102% | 20.4% |

### Notes

(1) Profit calculation as in (a)

(2) Average Investment = (opening cost or book value + closing book value)÷2 for mid-year value.

(3) Under the straight-line method of providing depreciation, the average investment value falls year by year giving rise to an increasing reported ROI throughout the life of the asset.

# Topflight

c) ii) and iii)

WORKINGS Number of passengers a year 3,438 @ contribution per passenger £(162.50-£25.00)

$$3,438 \times £137.50 = £472,725$$

Fixed costs (cash only) Servicing + Crew - Advertising revenue

$$£(45,000 + 90,000 - 25,000) = £110,000$$

Net annual cash flow from project TOPFLIGHT = £362,725

| Year | Cash flow (£) | Company target PV @ 15% | £ | Leisure Division target PV @ 17% | £ |
|---|---|---|---|---|---|
| 0 | -1,200,000 | 1.000 | -1,200,000 | 1.000 | -1,200,000 |
| 1 | + 362,725 | 0.870 | + 315,570 | 0.855 | + 310,129 |
| 2 | + 362,725 | 0.756 | + 274,220 | 0.730 | + 264,789 |
| 3 | + 362,725 | 0.657 | + 238,310 | 0.624 | + 226,340 |
| 4 | + 362,725 | 0.572 | + 207,478 | 0.534 | + 193,695 |
| 5 | + 362,725 | 0.497 | + 180,274 | 0.456 | + 165,402 |
| NPVs | + 613,625 | | + 15,852 | | - 39,645 |

Glenhall Limited is reporting a latest return on investment of £7.5 million ÷ £50 million = 15% and from this position any proposal showing an expected positive NPV at a cost of capital of 15% will improve the profits of the company. The project TOPFLIGHT does show a positive NPV for the company and acceptance of it will therefore benefit the shareholders in due course.

However, in order for the Leisure Division manager to participate in the bonus scheme, any new scheme must not decrease the current division ROI of 17%. The manager can see that the NPV is negative when the project cash flows are discounted at 17% and that the project targets in the first two years do not match the current ROI. Thus it seems unlikely that Leisure Division will accept this project because of it's detrimental effect on that division's performance measures and Glenhall Limited may lose an opportunity to increase its overall profitability.

SELECTED PERFORMANCE MEASURES

## Liquidity or Solvency

Short-term:

Acid Test

$$\frac{\text{Current assets capable of conversion into cash almost immediately}}{\text{Current liabilities due for payment almost immediately}}$$

Current Ratio                 $\dfrac{\text{Current assets}}{\text{Current liabilities}}$

Debtor collection            $\dfrac{\text{Debtors x 365 days}}{\text{Turnover (Sales)}}$
period

Creditor payment             $\dfrac{\text{Creditors x 365 days}}{\text{Cost of Sales*}}$        *Sales figure is used
period                                                                    where Cost of Sales
                                                                          figure is not
                                                                          available.

Stock turnover               $\dfrac{\text{Stock x 365 days}}{\text{Turnover (Sales)}}$
ratio

Longer-Term:

Gearing Ratio                $\dfrac{\text{Total loans}}{\text{Shareholders' funds}} \times 100\%$

Interest Cover               $\dfrac{\text{Profit before interest and taxation}}{\text{Interest payable in the year}}$

## Profitability

Return on net                $\dfrac{\text{Profit before interest and taxation}}{\text{Net assets (Fixed assets+net current assets)}}$
assets[†]

Return on sales              $\dfrac{\text{Profit before interest and taxation}}{\text{Turnover (Sales)}} \times 100\%$
(Profit margin)

Net asset turnover           $\dfrac{\text{Turnover (Sales)}}{\text{Net assets}}$

[†]     this ratio is also commonly known as return on capital employed
        (ROCE) and return on investment (ROI). Figures used for both
        the numerator (profit) and the denominator (net assets) can be
        varied to suit the circumstances of the organisation.

## Shareholders' measures

Dividend cover               $\dfrac{\text{Dividend payable x 100\%}}{\text{Profit after taxation}}$

Dividend yield               $\dfrac{\text{Dividend payable per ordinary share (in pence)}}{\text{Market price of ordinary share (in pence)}}$

Earnings per share           $\dfrac{\text{Profit after taxation}}{\text{Number of issued ordinary shares ranking for dividend payment}}$
(EPS)

- 57 -

| Price Earnings Ratio (P/E) | $\dfrac{\text{Market price of ordinary share (in pence)}}{\text{Earnings per share}}$ |
|---|---|

## Local Authorities' measures

| Gross recovery rate | $\dfrac{\text{Income} \times 100\%}{\text{All Expenditure}}$ | |
|---|---|---|
| Operational recovery rate | $\dfrac{\text{Income} \times 100\%}{\text{Operational Expenditure}}$ | where operational costs exclude loan charges, central management charges and rates. |
| Gross subsidy rate | Gross Expenditure less total income | |
| Gross subsidy rate per user | $\dfrac{\text{Gross Expenditure less total income}}{\text{Number of Attendances}}$ | |
| Operational subsidy | Total Operational Expenditure less total income | |
| Operational subsidy per user | $\dfrac{\text{Total Operational Expenditure less total income}}{\text{Number of Attendances}}$ | |
| Occupancy rate | $\dfrac{\text{Number of bookings made} \times 100\%}{\text{Total number of space bookings available}}$ | |
| Income measures | $\dfrac{\text{Income from activities} \times 100\%}{\text{Total Income}}$ | |
| | Income per activity area | |
| | Income per square metre | |
| | Income per hour | |
| Average spend per head | $\dfrac{\text{Income (Excluding bar/catering)}}{\text{Number of admissions}}$ | |
| Expenditure measures | $\dfrac{\text{Expenditure item} \times 100\%}{\text{Operational Expenditure}}$ | |
| Cost efficiency | $\dfrac{\text{Number of admissions}}{\text{Operational Expenditure}}$ | |
| Catering | $\dfrac{\text{Bar/Catering/Vending Gross Profit}}{\text{Bar/Catering/Vending Revenue}}$ | |
| Catering spend per head | $\dfrac{\text{Bar/Catering/Vending Income}}{\text{Number of admissions}}$ | |

## FURTHER READING

### General

MOTT G  *'Accounting for Non-Accountants'* 4th edition 1993

Covers the methods and techniques in common usage for financial decision making and financial control in the commercial sector.  No specific industry bias.

### Leisure and Recreation Management

GRATTON C &  *'Economics of Leisure Services Management'*
TAYLOR P       Longman/ILAM 1988

Includes a short discussion of investment appraisal at a Leisure Centre.

SCEATS A *'Sports and Leisure Club Management'* M & E Handbooks

Contains detailed advice on a wide range of operational management matters for sports and leisure clubs with coverage of financial control aspects.

### Charities

BLUME H & *'Accounting and Financial Management for Charities'*
NORTON M  Directory of Social Change

A basic guide for treasurers and managers in the charitable sector.

### Local Authorities

A wide range of publications exist on financial management in local authorities.  The reader is directed in particular to the Audit Commission for Local Authorities in England and Wales, the Accounts Commission for Scotland and The Chartered Institute of Public Finance and Accountancy (CIPFA) for their latest publications.

### Performance Indicators in Leisure and Recreation

Audit Commission relevant publications:

*'Preparing for Compulsory Competition'* 1989

*'Competitive Management of Parks and Open Spaces'* 1988

*'Sport for Whom?  Clarifying the Local Authority Role in Sport and Recreation'* 1989

CIPFA  *'Leisure and Recreation Statistics'* published annually

The Sports Council has a series of data sheets on CCT in relation to recreation management as well as other useful publications.

*'Management Paper Number 1 "Measuring Performance"'* 1988

Sets out suggestions for calculating recovery rates in sports and recreation facilities.

## Citizens' Charter

Under the Local Government Act 1992, the Audit Commission is required to determine a set of indicators for local authority services.

Audit Commission relevant publications (to date):

'The Citizen's Charter: Local Authority Performance Indicators' 1992

'Citizen's Charter Performance Indicators' 1992
(the consultation document) which led to

'Citizen's Charter Indicators: Charting a Course' 1992

which sets out the definitive information required for the first year 1993/94 of publication by authorities to a deadline of 31st December 1994.


## GLOSSARY OF TERMS

| | |
|---|---|
| Break even point | The output or activity level or sales value at which total costs equal total revenue. |
| Compulsory Competitive (CCT) | The process initiated by Statutory Instrument 1989 No. 2488, The Local Government Act 1988 (Competition in Sports and Leisure Facilities) Order 1989, whereby local authorities in England, Scotland and Wales are required to submit the management of leisure and recreation facilities to competitive tendering. Tender specifications are prepared by the authority as **client** and the successful bidder becomes the **contractor**. Employees of the authority frequently bid as a **Direct Services Organisation** (DSO). Central services costs previously allocated on an arbitrary basis become negotiable and written agreement to accept and pay for these services is contained in a **Service Level Agreement** (SLA). |
| Contribution | The difference between the sales value and the variable costs of those sales. |
| Debenture | A debt taken on by a company where details of interest payments, capital repayments and company assets promised as security for the loan are set out in a written legal agreement. |
| Depreciation | A proportion of the original cost of a fixed asset which is charged as an expense against income. |
| Fixed costs | Costs which will not change if the activity or output level changes within a specified time period. |
| Flexible budgets | A range of budgets showing the effect on revenues and costs of achieving various activity levels. |

| | |
|---|---|
| Franchise | A licence to sell a product or operate a service under a trademark name. |
| Limiting Factor | The key factor which restricts the growth of the organisation at the present time. |
| Margin of safety | The difference between the break-even level of activity and the actual (or budgeted) level of activity expressed as a % of the actual (or budgeted) level. |
| Net present value (NPV) | The sum of net yearly cash flows discounted back to time 0 at the cost of capital or other chosen discount rate. |
| Payback period | The length of time taken to recoup the original cash investment in a project. |
| Recovery rate | Revenue expressed as a % of expenditure. |
| Value for money (vfm) | The three concepts of economy, efficiency and effectiveness are components of value for money. |
| | **Economy:** how actual input costs compare with planned costs. |
| | **Efficiency:** output divided by resources consumed; or the cost of inputs divided by the output. |
| | **Effectiveness:** how far the output achieves the set objectives for the service. |
| | Where a precise measurement is available it is called a **performance measure**; where it cannot be measured precisely it may be possible to construct **performance indicators**. |
| Variable Costs | Costs which vary when the level of output or activity changes. |
| Working capital | Short-term assets and liabilities (commonly; stock, debtors, cash, trade creditors, other creditors, investments). |
| Writing down allowance (WDA) | A tax allowance on capital expenditure calculated by adding each asset to a 'pool' at its cost price and giving a WDA of 25% on the balance each year. |